Suzuki
Piano Ensemble Music
Volume 2   2 Pianos - 4 Hands
SECOND PIANO ACCOMPANIMENTS

by Barbara Meixner

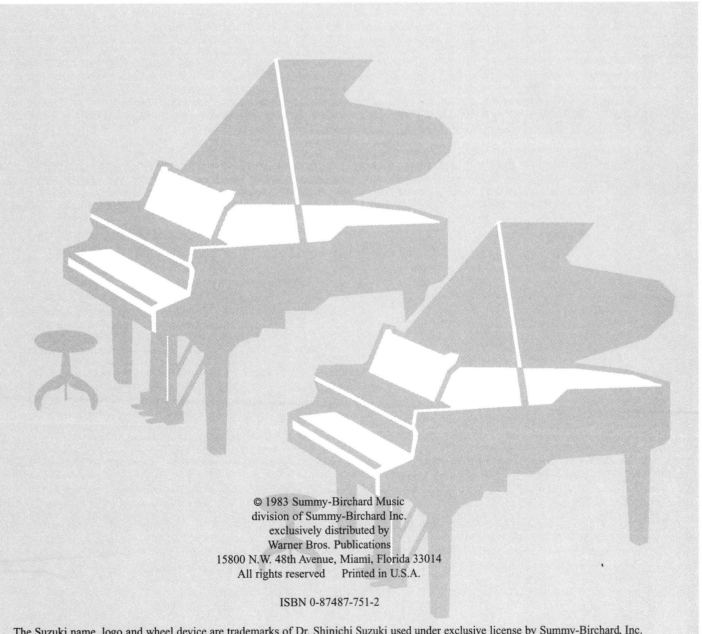

© 1983 Summy-Birchard Music
division of Summy-Birchard Inc.
exclusively distributed by
Warner Bros. Publications
15800 N.W. 48th Avenue, Miami, Florida 33014
All rights reserved   Printed in U.S.A.

ISBN 0-87487-751-2

CONTENTS

Ecossaise

J.N. Hummel

D.C.

A Short Story

H. Lichner

The Happy Farmer

Op. 68, No. 10
R. Schumann

Minuet 1
(From Suite in G Minor)

BWV 822
J.S. Bach

Allegretto

0751

Minuet 7
(From Suite in G Minor)

BWV822
J.S. Bach

Cradle Song

C.M. von Weber

Minuet, K.2

W.A. Mozart

Arietta

W.A. Mozart

18

poco rallent.

p a tempo

Melody

Op. 68, No. 1
R. Schumann

Sonatina in G

Anh. 5, No. 1
L. van Beethoven

Sonatina in G

Anh. 5, No. 1
L. van Beethoven

Romance

28

0751

Musette

(From English Suite No. 3)

J.S. Bach